About the Author

Miriam Fields-Babineau is a professional animal trainer and the author of
over 30 books on animal training; she also provides animals for media
productions. She has trained many dogs of different breeds and mixes in
her classes over the years. She designed the Comfort Trainer Head
Halter, All-in-One Training Leash and other animal training products. She
resides on a farm in Virginia with her husband, son and many beloved pets.

About Our Cover Dog

Meet Cooper, a Puggle puppy owned by Kelly
Williams of California. Cooper lists chewing, playing
fetch and general mischief-making among his favorite
activities. His owner says that he's discerning and
smart and really loves the attention of his human
family and all his new friends.

Puggle

By Miriam Fields-Babineau

Puggle Sherman enjoys chewing on his toys, performing tricks and eating "anything you put in front of him."

Kennel Club Books®, the country's only major publisher of dog books exclusively, proudly presents its *Designer Dog® Series* to celebrate the Puggle's coming-out party. Continuing in its bold effort to produce a unique line of dog books, Kennel Club Books® releases the first ever books on the specific designer-dog cross-breeds. The company has also released many *Special Limited Editions* and *Special Rare-Breed Editions* on various unusual breeds.

Visit the publisher's website at www.kennelclubbooks.com to read more about the unique library of books available to dog lovers around the world.

Acknowledgments

Thanks to the following owners of the dogs featured in this book: Becca Byrne, Chelle, Andre and Devina Calbert, the Lanzillotta family, Mary Meyers and Jeanette, Danielle and Dylan O'Neal.

Photography by:
Chelle Calbert

with additional photos by:
Tara Darling, Karen Taylor and Alice van Kempen.

KENNEL CLUB BOOKS®
Designer Dog®
SERIES

PUGGLE
ISBN: 1-59378-678-6

Copyright © 2007 · Kennel Club Books® A Division of BowTie, Inc.
40 Broad Street, Freehold, NJ 07728 USA
Printed in South Korea

Library of Congress Cataloging-in-Publication Data
Fields-Babineau, Miriam.
   Puggle / by Miriam Fields-Babineau.
      p. cm. — (Designer dog)
   ISBN-13: 978-1-59378-678-6
   ISBN-10: 1-59378-678-6
   1. Puggle. 1. Title.
   SF429.P92F54 2007
   636.76—dc22
                                    2007009780

10 9 8 7 6 5 4 3 2 1

Contents

Pug.

Beagle.

From two of America's favorite purebreds

What Is a
Puggle?

The name for a baby echidna (platypus) is "puggle." The echidna is the only marsupial in Australia that lays eggs instead of birthing live young. The female lays an egg, which is incubated in a pouch, much like a young kangaroo. Ten days later the newborn hatches and is then considered a tiny puggle at less than half an inch long and weighing not even a thousandth of a pound. The puggle is carried in its mother's pouch until it begins growing spines, at which time his mom leaves him in a burrow and returns every few days to feed him. The puggle leaves his burrow at the age of six months and his mom weans him around four months later.

Now for the canine version (far cuter than a platypus): a Puggle is the offspring of breeding a male Pug with a female Beagle.

There are well over 400 breeds of dog, many recognized by kennel clubs throughout the world. Many breeds are still in their infancy as breeders try to standardize their dogs to fit specific size and behavior guidelines. Now comes the designer-dog craze. This puts a wrinkle in the fabric of the purebred dog world, as hybrids and mixed breeds are becoming as popular and desirable as purebred dogs. Moreover, their price tags are often higher than those of purebreds.

Designer dogs are also called hybrids—a combination of two purebred dogs. The mixture can be any combination of the known

comes one of today's favorite hybrids.

Pet owners are attracted to Puggles for their compact size and companion qualities.

registered breeds. The most popular hybrid dogs have been those mixed with Poodles, such as the Labradoodle, Golden-doodle, Cockapoo and others. Pug crosses are the latest hybrids to join the scene, and the Puggle is quickly gaining ground as it becomes the hybrid of choice among the fashionably elite, such as film and television celebrities. The *New York Post* has compared the Puggle to the equivalent of breeding a Marc Jacobs bag to a Louis Vuitton handbag, as the price of one of these designer bags is very much the same as the price of a Puggle—anywhere from $600 to $2000. Granted, a Puggle is not a handbag, but the dog's size is similar to that of a larger designer bag, and the hybrid suits the lifestyles of many who live in urban areas.

Wallace Havens is the first person to have purposely bred Beagles and Pugs together. He has been breeding hybrids since 1967. Though hybrids such as Cockapoos have been around for decades, the Puggle idea

Puggles love to take life by the reins.

actually occurred by chance. A customer came to Mr. Havens's Puppy Haven Kennel and told him of an accidental breeding between a Pug and a Beagle. He related how he'd seen the puppies and they were very cute. The customer suggested that Havens give the combination a try.

So, in 1993, the first Puggle puppies were sold at Barking Lot Pet Shop in Milwaukee, Wisconsin. Since this first litter, Wallace Havens has sold a rabble of Puggle puppies to pet shops and directly to customers around the country.

David Dietz, who resides in Brooklyn, New York, has been selling Havens's Puggles for nearly a decade. He claims to sell upwards of 500 hybrid dogs per year. Dietz says that many people come into his store to buy another breed, but once they see the Puggle they are instantly infatuated with its appearance and personality. He says that men are attracted to the Puggle's activity level. The dog loves to run and play outside, though tends to be quiet indoors. Women like the Puggle's endearing face, with the big eyes and wrinkled fore-head. Children love the dog because he is small, affection-ate and playful. Puggles also love nothing more than to curl up on a lap for a snooze, and nobody can resist that. More-over, they love to impress their human companions.

"They say I have my
mother's ears."

Of all the toy hybrid dogs, Puggles are among the most sturdy while also being compact. Mike Rubin, who has worked with Puggles for years, says they're ideal pets for children. They have great dispositions and inquisitive minds. Rubin tells his Puggle-owning clients that the dogs must be given regular exercise such as walks or trips to the dog park to expend their energy and that they should be trained in order to be good companions. He has sold Puggles to many celebrities, as this hybrid dog easily fits within their lifestyles. The list of Puggle-owning celebrities is a virtual who's who, including James Gandolfini, Sylvester Stallone and Jake Gyllenhaal.

Rubin claims that though the Puggle is half Pug, he rarely has the respiratory issues commonly related to the Pug

It's fun to snuggle with a Puggle (or two).

breed because the Beagle traits give the Puggle a longer nose, though still rounded and cute. The Puggle's short coat is easy to maintain, and his size makes him easy to bring along with you.

Why would a dog owner choose a Puggle instead of a purebred Beagle or Pug? Let's look at the two parent breeds more closely and discover why this little hybrid has stolen hearts and emptied wallets.

THE BEAGLE

Beagles are popular pets and great hunting dogs. They have energy, willingness and great dispositions. They originated in England as a cross between the Harrier and other hounds. Beagles can hunt in packs, alone or in pairs. The most common use of a Beagle is as a rabbit-hunting dog, though they also track quail and pheasant equally well. Because Beagles have incredible scenting abilities, they are currently being used as narcotic-detection dogs in airports and at border checkpoints. They have also been trained to detect bomb-building materials and other contraband. Their small size and cuteness make them less menacing in appearance than the usual police dogs and their noses are unsurpassed.

Beagles are sturdy and squarely built. They come in two small sizes, either 13 inches or under at the shoulder or over 13 but under 15 inches at the shoulder. They weigh around 18–25 pounds, though they are "food hounds" and can easily become overweight, reaching 40 pounds or more. Beagle coat colors are usually a combination of white, brown and black, with the black forming a saddle over the back and the white normally encasing the legs, chest, neck and nose. Some Beagles are lemon-colored with white; the lemon coloring is either in patches or in a saddle-like pattern as in the typical tri-colored Beagle. Beagles have short, easy-care coats but they do tend to shed—a lot. Aside from brushing, Beagles don't require much grooming other than consistent cleaning of their fold-over ears to prevent ear infections and regular trimming of their nails.

Beagles have broad skulls and slightly rounded straight muzzles. They have strong wide feet, great for traversing any terrain. Their eyes are hazel brown, their ears long, soft and pendant. They normally carry their straight tails high, but never over their backs. Their black noses with wide full nostrils are built for scenting. Beagles were bred as scenting hounds, and not many other dogs can surpass this breed's ability to track game and stay on a trail for extended periods of time. They have a distinct loud howl/bay that alerts their human hunting companions to the location of their quarry.

Due to the Beagle's (shown here) head traits, the Puggle offspring have longer muzzles and less wrinkling than a purebred Pug.

This medium to small breed has a good life expectancy at 12–15 years. Long life expectancy makes the hybrid pups more attractive to potential buyers. The average litter size is 7, though as many as 14 pups can be born to one mother.

There are some lines of Beagles that are prone to certain health problems, which include heart disease, eye and back problems and chondrodysplasia (dwarfism). But, when compared to the problems that are found in many other breeds, such as the popular retrievers or spaniels, the number of potential health issues found in the Beagle is relatively minor.

Beagles have great temperaments. They're sweet, curious and lively, and are very social with other dogs and people. In fact, they love people so much that they can easily develop separation anxiety if left alone for long periods of time. Beagle owners who have long work hours often have more than one dog so that they have the company of each other.

Because Beagles are hunting hounds, they do have a huge prey drive. Beagles are difficult to control if they catch the scent of other animals, as their instincts take over 100%. This attribute might make them difficult companions in households that have cats or other small pets.

This breed also requires a lot of exercise. While their size is ideal for life in a condominium or apartment-style community, they do need to be allowed regular opportunities to run, play and socialize. Without this, they can become very destructive.

Beagles are very determined, stubborn and alert, a combination that can make them difficult to train for anyone who doesn't have patience, persistence and the willingness to be consistent at all times.

THE PUG

The American Kennel Club classifies the Pug as a toy breed, though it was actually originally derived from a giant breed, the Mastiff. There are mixed thoughts on this history, as the Pug is a very old breed, having been recognized as early

The Puggle's coloration is similar to that of the Pug, although black Puggles are more rare than black Pugs.

as 400 BC in Asia. In the 16th century Pugs were fashionable in the European courts, reaching a peak of popularity during the Victorian era. This breed was favored in Tibet at monasteries and later traveled to Japan, where it became equally popular.

There are some historical events of note in the Pug's background. In 1572 a Pug saved the life of William, Prince of Orange, by alerting him to approaching Spaniards at Hermingny. Josephine, wife of Napoleon, sent secret messages to her husband under the collar of her Pug while she was imprisoned. When the British conquered the Chinese Imperial Palace in 1860, they discovered several Pugs and brought them back to England with them. The American Kennel Club recognized the breed very early, in 1885, though the world had already known of their superior watchdog and performance abilities for many hundreds of years.

Pugs are square, thick set, stocky and compact. Their ears are rose shaped, their legs are straight and strong and their tails are curled tightly over their backs. When they walk, they have a jaunty, rolling gait that's very distinctive; the Beagle, on the other hand, trots and lopes. Pugs are about 10–11 inches tall and weigh around 14–18 pounds. As with Beagles, though, Pugs love to eat and require weight-watching from an early age.

Pugs come in apricot-fawn or silver with a black muzzle, or solid black. This is a brachycephalic (short-muzzled) breed with big, bulging eyes that are low set. Most Pugs have moles on their cheeks, giving them high-fashion beauty marks. Their coats are short, smooth and easy to groom, but like Beagles, Pugs shed a lot. Their wrinkled faces require extra attention in cleaning between the creases to prevent skin infections. As this is a toy breed, Pugs are sensitive to extreme weather conditions. They should never be allowed outdoors when wet and must always be covered when going out into the cold. In hot weather they can have trouble breathing and can overheat easily, so they must be kept cool. In the heat, they should always be in well-ventilated spaces and in air-conditioned spaces whenever possible.

Pugs tend to have more health problems than Beagles, so the Puggle offers the possibility of reduced health risks for the hybrid offspring. The most common health problems in Pugs are eye problems such as keratitis (inflammation of the cornea) and corneal ulcers and chronic breathing problems due to their short, pushed-in noses. Their short muzzles also make them prone to snoring, wheezing and temperature-related reactions. The Pug is also prone to skin problems.

For those living in small spaces, the Pug is ideal. Pugs are not highly active dogs, though they will run and play outdoors when given the chance. If living in an apartment, a Pug is relatively happy to just race around indoors for a short time and then take a nap. In fact, Pugs are big nappers.

As for temperament, Pugs compare closely to Beagles. They are loyal, affectionate and happy, albeit willful. They love to socialize with people and other dogs, and nobody is a stranger. Pugs are also sensitive and intelligent. They will bore easily and must be stimulated by learning new things or playing new games. They love training, providing it is done in a positive manner, for they will quickly shut down if treated harshly.

The Puggle's soulful eyes and wrinkled face have captured
many a heart.

Pugs live well with other dogs, cats and small pets. They don't have the high prey drive of Beagles and they can easily be distracted into another activity. Pugs are good watchdogs and will alert their owners to an unknown presence, though they are not overly yappy like many toy breeds.

Puggle fanciers feel that this hybrid contains the best of Pug and Beagle worlds.

ENTER THE PUGGLE

Let's look at what happens when we bring the Pug and Beagle together. Because both individual breeds have similar attributes, the Puggle isn't drastically different from the parent breeds in size or temperament. Also as with the parent breeds, this little dog is long lived, typically reaching 15 years.

The Puggle does differ in appearance from the Pug and the Beagle. Puggles are about 13–15 inches tall at the shoulder and weigh an average of 15–30 pounds. However, there is such a thing as a Pocket Puggle, where the dam is a small Olde English Pocket Beagle, weighing only 8–12 pounds, which makes the pups quite small.

Puggles are energetic little dogs with short fawn or tan coats, black faces and wrinkled foreheads. Their legs are short, stocky and straight. Most have tails that curl upward, some over their backs. Their ears droop or fold over. Unlike the Pug, the Puggle's eyes don't bulge outward, but they are still large, dark, liquid, soulful eyes that steal many hearts.

The Puggle's short coat requires little care besides regular brushing, and other grooming tasks are minimal: the typical cleaning of ears and clipping of nails. Those Puggles with very wrinkled foreheads should have the creases cleaned to prevent skin infections, to which this hybrid is prone. Because he sheds a lot, the Puggle is not the dog for those with allergies or for people who don't like vacuuming.

Puggles inherit their temperament from both parent breeds, and both the Beagle and the Pug are friendly, loving and great with other dogs. With a Puggle, nobody is a stranger, and being a lap dog is the ultimate luxury. Puggles love nothing more than to curl up and cuddle, though they do have a lot of energy when they play. Their gait, a combination of rolling and trotting, is funny to watch and their expressions are priceless.

Puggles are willful, a trait they inherit from the hound side, but their intelligence

Wave hello to a hybrid who's exploded onto the designer-dog scene.

makes the training process fairly easy. They can learn any command and can perform tricks very well. House-training is often an issue, though, as their small size can make their human companions lax with the rules. Yes, their droppings may be small, but they need to be potty-trained just like any other dog. Puggles can easily learn to do their business outside or in a litterbox indoors.

If you've "got Puggles," then you've g

Pug + *Beagle* =
Puggle

Puggles have been around since the early 1990s, but there has not been any type of standardization of the hybrid mixture. Puggles became very popular very quickly. Hence, breeders popped up everywhere with few restrictions on or expectations of what they produced.

The intent behind the Puggle, as it is with hybrids in general, is to bring together two breeds of dog that are attractive and have appealing personalities. Many hybrids are small dogs, as people want dogs that are easily cared for in an urban or suburban environment. Other considerations include producing hybrid puppies that are unlikely to have the inherited defects so commonly found in purebred dogs.

Though Puggles have similar characteristics—most are fawn to red in color with dark faces—the Puggle cannot be

Designer dog, designer style.

plenty of canine affection and fun.

COMMON PUGGLE HEALTH AILMENTS

Hip dysplasia

A painful condition in which the head of the thigh bone and the socket of the hip do not fit together properly.

Hypothyroidism

A disorder in which the thyroid gland is underactive, affecting metabolism and other body functions.

Patellar luxation

Also called "slipped kneecaps," a condition in which the kneecaps pop out of place.

Legg-Calve-Perthes disease

A disorder of the blood supply to the head of the thigh bone, causing death of the bone and arthritis of the hip.

General eye problems

considered a breed. Puggles must be created by breeding a Pug to a Beagle. Moreover, the sire must be the Pug and the dam the Beagle. Otherwise, the offspring appear more Pug-like with bulging eyes and very short noses; both of these physical constructions are prone to health problems, as the eyes are easily injured and short noses often lead to respiratory issues.

People who breed together two different breeds of dog are not only looking for a "designer-dog" appearance but also to produce a dog with fewer genetic defects. The idea is that the larger the gene pool, the lower the percentage of inherited problems. This is called the "heterosis effect," defined as physical or mental strength, force or energy, also termed "hybrid vigor." Though many hybrid dog breeders have been lucky with the reduction of the occurrence of genetic defects, they do still occur. Recessive genes have a way of popping up from time to time. While a good breeder will refrain from rebreeding a dog

Puggles are active dogs, but they thoroughly enjoy relaxation time, too.

It didn't take the Puggle long to make a splash from sea to shining sea!

A trait surely inherited from both parent breeds is a Puggle's love of food.

that has produced pups with genetic defects, there are many unscrupulous breeders who won't, as they care more about cashing in on the designer-dog craze than about producing quality pups.

Crossing pure-bred dogs doesn't always create offspring with similar features. The pups can be any combination of the parents' genes, so one rarely knows the actual size or temperament of the pups until they are fully grown. While the majority of Puggles don't mature to more than 20 pounds, there are some that can weigh up to 40 pounds and stand 16 inches at the shoulder. A person who purchases a designer dog is still taking the chance that his pup will be more like one of the parents rather than a 50-50 combination of both parents.

Many hybrid dogs can be a simple F_1 generation (one purebred bred to another purebred), which is said to produce the best hybrid vigor. An F_1 generation hybrid bred back to one of the parent breeds is often done to achieve a specific characteristic. This would be called an F_1b generation. When breeding two hybrids together, the offspring is considered an F_2 generation. The generations can be further crossed by creating an F_2b backcross or even breeding two F_2 generation dogs together. This has been done with Labradoodles in order to create a standardized appearance so that they would be recognizable as an actual breed instead of a hybrid. After 15 years of selective breeding, Labradoodles are now more often crossed with each other than with purebred Labrador Retrievers or Poodles, though on occasion they are bred back to one of the parent breeds.

Puggle breeders don't do multi-generational crossing. They maintain the F_1 generation by crossing Pug males with Beagle females in order to obtain the preferred characteristics: wrinkled forehead, short but not snubbed snout, curly tail, short fur and large but not bulging eyes. These traits, along with their playful, loving personalities, keep the dogs attractive to prospective buyers. Good Puggle breeders choose the parents for good temperament and size, in addition to specifically breeding Beagle females to Pug males.

Irresistible Puggle puppies grow up into attractive adults.

Puggles love to be

Snuggle
Puggle

As the Pug and the Beagle

share many character traits, combining the two breeds does not do much to change the intrinsic nature of either breed in the offspring. We've mentioned that both breeds are eager to please, loyal, hard-working, fairly active dogs who learn quickly. Nobody is a stranger to either breed, and both will "sound the alarm" when it comes to alerting their owners to intrusions on their property or friends approaching.

A Puggle can always find a place to snuggle.

right where their owners are.

Like his Beagle ancestors, a Puggle is sure to follow his nose.

Puggles are great with children, although their energy may be too much for young children. Puggles are always very willing to cuddle with youngsters, though. Older children often do well with Puggles because the dogs are happy to romp and play for long periods of time. They don't mind a slight amount of rough and tumble, nor do they get mouthy or pushy. In fact, there is hardly a Puggle that has shown any aggressive tendencies, even when frightened.

Puggles are very social. They easily accept other dogs and new people. In fact, they welcome newcomers into the pack with delight. Although a

A designer wardrobe for a designer dog... a sweater for a Puggle in cold weather is both fashionable and functional.

Puggle may bark when a stranger is near his home, he will not go into any type of "attack mode." As soon as he has a chance to sniff the stranger, that person or animal is welcomed. A Puggle can't be counted on to protect home and family unless the intruder is intimidated by the mere sound of the canine.

Puggles are intelligent. Shown how to do something a few times, they have a good understanding of the exercise and delight in performing it. In fact, they love to show off. It's rare to go through a day with a Puggle and not laugh at his antics or be amazed by what he can do.

Ready to play with a friend...

...or with a toy.

With these characteristics, Puggles have a tendency to outfox their owners if not trained and guided. This is typical of any intelligent animal who learns how to get what he wants through a little ingenuity. A Puggle will try displaying a certain behavior and, if rewarded in some manner, he will continue to perform this behavior. Puggle owners must train their dogs! Training brings harmony. The dog will learn proper guidelines and happily abide by them.

Physically, Puggles are fairly sturdy dogs, but they cannot withstand extreme temperatures for long periods of time without protection. Have fun choosing a Puggle wardrobe, as they do need winter coats when going out in the cold. In extreme heat, don't allow the Puggle to exercise outside without plenty of water and access to shade. This is not necessarily due to their breed combination but more to their size, as small dogs do not have the same ability to control their body temperatures as larger dogs. While their short coats are helpful in keeping them cooler in warmer climates, it doesn't do them any favors in cold climates.

In many breeds a particular sex might be preferred to ensure desired characteristics.

The Ideal Family for a Puggle:

- Gives the dog outdoor walks (in addition to potty trips) or playtime at least once per day
- Takes the time to train and stimulate their dog
- Continually offers positive reinforcement and new stimuli in the dog's environment
- Spends a lot of time with their dog; Puggles thrive on attention
- Gives the dog time to play with other dogs; this hybrid is very social
- Maintains a regular daily routine and schedule
- Has children in the family who love the dog

Your Puggle can't wait for you to get home!

For example, many female dogs tend to be easier to train, while male dogs might be more territorial. Puggles also tend to have sex-specific temperaments. The male Puggle is a little lazy and laid-back, while the female Puggle is more inquisitive, energetic and eager to be involved in family activities. Both are great watchdogs; if you live in an apartment community, it will be important to train your Puggle not to bark at every little sound, only when someone is actually at your door.

Keeping in mind the Puggle's behavior characteristics, we must consider who would make an ideal Puggle owner. This isn't a dog for everyone. An active family who has the time and desire to include the dog in their daily routines is a perfect home for a Puggle. This is a dog who needs attention and company. Puggles may become very depressed if left alone for long periods of time, especially if crated. If you're busy, the little dog will happily trot by your side or sit under your chair, or,

LIFESTYLE CHOICES

Dogs are often chosen to fill the gaps in our fast-paced lives. Americans are having children later in life or sometimes not having any at all. Dogs are fulfilling people's need to have "someone" to nurture. Just as the allure of designer clothing grabs our attention, the ability to own a unique or rare type of dog has become a symbol of success.

However, as many people are becoming aware, dogs are not pieces of furniture to just sit in a room and look nice, nor are they clothing that can be put away in the closet when you no longer wish to wear it. Dogs need attention, care and training. They require much of their human companions' time, especially those dogs that have the blood of high-activity breeds running through their veins.

Designer dogs are becoming more prominent at animal shelters and rescue groups, without the high price tag, as those people with busy lifestyles who wanted canine status symbols are throwing the dogs away just as they would discard items of clothing that are taking up space in the dresser.

preferably, sit in your lap. A Puggle who spends too much time alone is likely to become destructive and develop separation anxiety.

Puggles thrive on routine, knowing what will happen and when. Without this, they might develop behavioral problems, for their lives will be inconsistent. Inconsistency creates insecurity. Maintaining specific feeding and exercise times will help this hybrid be more relaxed.

A trained Puggle is safe at home alone for short periods of time. Your Puggle will learn quickly if taught in a positive manner. Without rewards for doing the right things, however, he may behave in an undesirable way because it earns him attention, even if it's not positive attention. Puggles are attention hogs. They will quickly learn how to attain attention of any type. It is up to you, as the Puggle owner, to guide your dog in the right direction. Don't sit and complain. Train and explain. Your Puggle will not fail to show off and make you laugh.

The Non-ideal Family for a Puggle:

• Is rarely home
• Does not offer the dog any stimulation in the form of play or training
• Does not train the dog
• Does not allow the dog time to play with other dogs
• Has a family member with allergic reactions to dog hair and dander
• Has neighbors who will not tolerate barking

The best thing you can give your Puggle is affection...
and more affection.

Irresistible Puggle puppies

The ideal Puggle is outgoing

and happy-go-lucky. He's a dog who willingly comes to you, but doesn't overwhelm you by nipping at you or climbing on you. Puggles are energetic, bouncy and playful, yet they are also quiet lap dogs who will happily sleep and cuddle with you. Some, however, can be quite stubborn, as both of their parents have that tendency.

A pup with good conformation has a body type similar to a Beagle, though lighter boned. He will be slightly longer than he is tall, whereas a Pug is more squarely formed. The pup will have a curly tail, a round head and a sharp stop at the forehead. The head is very "Pug-like," although not as big and round. A long Beagle-type nose should be avoided. The ears should be of light leather, droopy and cute, with the tips not extending past the jawline. The pup's nose should be short and square.

The Puggle is considered a toy dog like the Pug. Small dogs have enjoyed a recent surge in popularity due to their portability. Many owners also enjoy the wide variety of designer pooch carriers that have become fashionable for small dogs. Just pick him up and go!

The price of a Puggle varies according to the dog's conformation, color and desired traits. Black Puggles are rare, so they normally have a higher price tag. Most Puggles run from $600 to

make it hard to choose!

A black Puggle is a rare and more expensive find.

$2,000 each (depending on where you purchase the pup), with Pocket Puggles on the higher side due to their being rare and desirable.

Ideally all of the puppies in a litter are kept together until eight weeks of age. This gives the young dogs a chance to learn early social skills, which will help them form well-adjusted personalities and welcome other animals and people. Removal from the litter before eight weeks of age can cause serious behavioral issues later. Further, puppies should not be shipped before eight to ten weeks of age.

The litter of Puggles should be registered with the American Canine Hybrid Club, located in Arkansas. This is important because the ACHC only registers litters with two purebred parents.

Here's a list of questions to consider:

1. Where am I buying my Puggle? If directly from the breeder, the pups will have had the advantage of being raised in a home environment. A good breeder is very concerned about the well-being of the puppies. If purchasing your puppy from a pet shop, inquire about the

origin of the puppies, their health, the age at which they left the breeder and whether their parents are AKC-registered.

2. If buying your puppy directly from a breeder or kennel, ask to see photos of the parents or to meet the parents if they are on the premises. Knowing the behavior of the parents will tell you a lot about the future personality of your dog.

3. Ask which vaccinations and worming treatments the puppies have or will receive. All health records should be available, regardless of where you buy your puppy.

4. Does the breeder or seller offer a guarantee? Whenever purchasing a puppy, a health guarantee is a no-brainer, though few Puggle owners return their pups to the seller regardless of the reasons, as it's love at first sight.

After checking for the health clearances and vaccinations and looking over the puppy's overall appearance and condition, the next step is temperament testing. There are several simple things you can do to assure that you take home the best Puggle puppy for your family and lifestyle.

Begin by taking the pup into a quiet area where there are few distractions. This will ensure that his reactions are true to his personality. Distractions will reflect in his responses, giving you incorrect information.

Test #1: Follow the Leader Crouch low and walk backward, clapping your hands softly. Most Puggles will come running to you because they are forward and

The typical Puggle look is tan/fawn with a black muzzle and wrinkles on the face.

Good Puggle breeders want the best for each and every one of their pups.

allows this without trying to squirm away or put his mouth on you, he is a good candidate and you can go on to the next test.

Test #3: Sound the Alert
Drop something, such as your keys, a bone or a book. The Puggle pup should be curious about the object. He shouldn't run away; he might even go up to it to check it out. As Pugs have long been known as alerting dogs, a Puggle might bark at the sound. If the pup runs away, he may not be a good choice, especially if you live in an apartment or condominium where there tends to be a lot of noise as people come and go.

Test #4: Roly Poly
Roll your puppy over onto his back. Hold him there for a few seconds. As you hold him, rub his tummy. A good prospect will lie quietly; if he gets a tummy rub for it, he'll quickly learn how to earn that reward. If the pup gets squirmy, gets mouthy or gets up, he will not be a good pup to put into a family with children.

friendly. If a pup doesn't respond in such a manner, cross him off your list.

Test #2: Touchy Feely
Touch your puppy all over. Take special care to touch his paws, ears and tail. If the pup

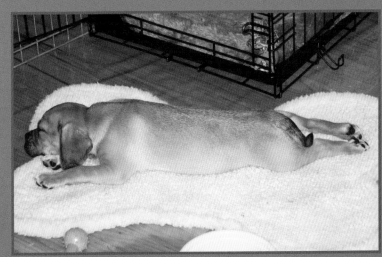

Every Puggle needs some room to stretch his legs.

Bundled up and ready to brave the cold.

Importance of Health Clearances

Regardless if you are buying a dog of purebred or mixed-breed heritage, it is important to see the parents' health clearances. Parents with good hearts, eyes clear of cataracts and well-structured hips will help the pup's buyer feel better about the overall health of the puppy he intends to purchase.

Be certain to request viewing the Orthopedic Foundation for Animals (OFA) and Canine Eye Registration Foundation (CERF) certifications on both parents. The hips should be tested as Good or Excellent. The eyes must be cataract-free and free from other common canine genetic problems, and the heart strong and healthy. Never purchase a puppy from a breeder without having seen the parents' clearances!

If you obtain your mixed-breed dog through a shelter, humane society or rescue group, you will almost never have the opportunity to view, or even know, anything about the parents. Be aware, however, that many mixed breeds can be healthier than many purebreds, as one parent's genes can counterbalance the recessive genes for disease in the other parent.

Test #5: Hi There

Expose the pup to other animals such as other dogs, cats and other pets. Puggles tend to welcome other creatures of all types, rarely showing aggression toward anything. However, this does not preclude their wanting to play with their new friends.

Once your pup has passed all the tests, you'll feel confident in your choice. Make sure you're ready for this energetic, loving and loyal dog.

SHELTER MY IMAGINATION

There are more purebreds and mixed-breed dogs at animal shelters than you can imagine. Visiting a shelter will both break your heart and open you up to the love of a dog. Most of the canine residents are adults, and few will find homes in time to save their lives.

Most busy households simply do not have the time to house-train a puppy. Adopting an adult dog from the shelter becomes a great option, as dogs over the age of six months can contain themselves longer than a pup, thus possibly being easier to house-train. Some adult dogs who have been turned over to shelters by their owners may already be house-trained. Many older dogs merely need a warm rug or foot to lie upon and are less demanding companions than the high-energy puppy who is always on the go.

Imagine the life that you can save and enjoy when obtaining an adult dog from a shelter.

Puggles are always

Caring for Your
Puggle

There's really not a whole lot of difference between raising a Puggle and raising any other common breed of dog. As a household companion, your Puggle needs to be kept clean and healthy, given proper nutrition and receive adequate exercise, training and education.

The first thing that you should do upon getting your new Puggle puppy is visit a veterinarian. The little guy will need a thorough physical examination, a fecal test to check for parasites and to be set up with a vaccination schedule that includes parvovirus, influenza, leptospirosis, distemper, coronavirus and bordetella (kennel cough). He should also be scheduled for his rabies vaccination, which is normally done at the age of four months. You'll also need to ask your vet about safe heartworm and flea and tick preventives, each usually administered in monthly doses.

GROOMING

Puggles are easy to maintain. Dirt and debris easily brush off their short coats, and they dry quickly after a bath or if they get wet outdoors. However, since your Puggle is a house dog, you'll want to bathe him as needed to keep him from developing a doggy odor. Both parents, the Pug and the Beagle, tend to have

ready for mealtime!

Puggle puppy, ready to clean up his act.

heavy doggy odor, making them unpleasant as lap dogs unless bathed and brushed regularly. And, unlike many of the Poodle-cross hybrid dogs, Puggles do shed quite a bit.

You won't need to spend a lot of time brushing your Puggle's coat. It is short, without any feathering or chance of matting. As pups tend to get into dirty mischief, and Puggles do love dirt (some even enjoy mud puddles), you will have to clean your dog off from time to time before he comes into the house. Obviously, he must be a part of the family and welcome in your home. Why else would you have a Puggle?

If your Puggle requires frequent baths, his skin and coat will benefit from omega fatty acid supplements and coat conditioner; both of these prevent the skin and coat from getting too dry, which can happen as a result of bathing often. While the Puggle's Beagle ancestry offers few skin problems, the Pug side does tend to have dry skin and requires careful attention to the skin folds. The folds need to be kept clean and dry or they will develop fungal infections. While most adult

Puggles tend to outgrow their forehead wrinkles, some don't. You'll need to give these skin folds special attention throughout your dog's life.

FEEDING

Puggle breeders suggest a high-protein diet for their pups, as they mature fairly quickly and need the nutrients that only a high-quality food can provide. While many toy-dog breeders suggest home-made diets of fresh meats, rice and vegetables supplemented with vitamins, there are some good commercial diets available that offer similar complete nutrition.

Prior to purchasing a packaged dog food, you'll want to read the ingredients. The first three to five ingredients listed are the main constitution of the food. If you see anything with corn, wheat, by-products or rice hulls in these first five ingredients, steer clear. Also, if you see more than three grains in the food, it means the food is mainly grain and not meat. Read on and check for food colorings, preservatives, additives and digest (stomach contents of the animals used in the food). Check the label for protein levels, as these are important when raising a fast-growing puppy. Some breeders suggest a protein level below 50% for both regular food and treats, as this will aid the dog in growing at a more even pace instead of having the risk of developing growing pains, a

Frequent brushing is part of a Puggle owner's routine.

A Designer Diet for All Dogs

Few dogs thrive on corn-based diets. You will rarely see a dog choose an ear of corn over a piece of meat. Dogs are omnivorous but require a good majority of their food to be meat-based. A quality dog food should contain meat as the main ingredient, and the remaining ingredients should include vegetables, brewer's yeast/rice, vitamins and omega fatty acids. Preservatives are not only a sign that rancid ingredients were used in the manufacturing of the food but can also be damaging, over time, to your dog's internal organs.

Veterinarians and breeders will normally steer their clients either to the brand they sell or have been using with their own dogs. Few will describe why that particular food is one they recommend. What are the key nutrients? Why will this particular food give the dog a glowing coat and spring in his step?

The easiest means of choosing a food is to read the label. The first three ingredients are those that comprise the majority of the food. You should see actual meat within the first three ingredients, meaning beef, chicken, lamb, fish or venison, not meal or corn or rice hulls. Actual meat. If you have a dog with meat allergies, try a fish- or venison-based diet.

Meat, it's what's for dinner!

condition in which the bones and muscles can't keep up with each other, causing lameness. However, this isn't as common with small dogs as it is with larger ones.

When using a commercial food, be sure to feed both canned and dry. The dry food, while good for the teeth and gums, is more processed than the canned food, meaning there are fewer vitamins. Canned food doesn't have to be processed as much, as the preserving factor of the canning process maintains the vitamins and moisture. That being said, dogs don't get 100% of their moisture from drinking water. A good percentage of it comes from the foods they eat, which is why it's a good idea to make

canned food a part of your Puggles' total diet. Not only will he receive better nutrition but he will also eat readily at mealtimes, making it easier to stick to a feeding schedule and thus a potty schedule.

EXERCISE
Puggles can easily adjust to any living environment, provided they receive proper

The Puggle's favorite type of exercise is anything he can do with you.

Puggle Safety

Safety precautions necessary for dog owners are very similar to those taken by parents of infants and young children. Begin with dog-proofing the rooms in which your puppy will be allowed to run and play. Do this *before* you even bring the puppy home. If your kitchen is to become the puppy room, make certain that the puppy can't get into any house-cleaning materials on shelves, in cabinets, etc. The same applies outside your home in the area of your yard where you intend to take the puppy for house-training. Make sure no plants (indoors and outdoors) are within easy puppy reach, as some plants are toxic and you can be sure that the pup will want to taste them if he can. A listing of toxic plants and other unsafe substances for dogs is available on the Animal Poison Control Center page of the ASPCA's website (*www.aspca.org*). Also, remove fallen branches from the yard and make sure that your Puggle doesn't drink from puddles or other unsafe sources of water. Puppies are curious creatures, so when it comes to safety, it is always better to be safe than to be sorry!

exercise. A Puggle will get some activity racing around the apartment or house a couple of times a day, but he needs to get out in the fresh air for exercise, not just for bathroom trips. This means regular daily walks and, if a fenced-in area is available, off-leash playtime. Puggles need to socialize with other dogs on a regular basis, so check out dog parks in your area or have doggie "play dates" with friends and their dogs. Social time with other canines aids in a dog's own behavior as well as giving him the type of exercise that simply cannot be fulfilled by his human companions.

Puggles tend to become very attached to their people and might develop separation anxiety issues if away from you for too long. If you must spend long hours away from home during the work week, having two Puggles might be the ticket so that they can keep each other company—though this hybrid does tend to have jealousy issues. Another option is to find a doggie daycare center near you. Allow your Puggle to go to doggie daycare at least three times per week (more, if possible). This energetic, willful hybrid will not do well cooped up for long periods of time in a small space by himself. If you cannot locate a doggie daycare, hire a dog walker or find a neighbor who would be willing to spend a few hours with your dog during the day. Who could resist a Puggle? Certainly not anyone who meets him!

Your Puggle thrives on attention and interactive play with his owners. If you take him for walks and play games with him, he will get more exercise and be more likely to relieve himself where he is supposed to. As both of the parent breeds have a propensity toward obesity, plenty of exercise will prevent your Puggle's becoming overweight. Obesity can greatly shorten a dog's lifespan. Good-quality food and lots of exercise will give you a healthy and happy Puggle to snuggle.

Aside from his owner,

Puggle

You already know about
hybrid vigor, although not in great detail. It has long
been said by many people, including some breeders and
veterinarians, that mutts make the best pets. They are
long-lived, are usually healthy and do not seem to have as many
inherited or genetic maladies as are seen in many of the purebred
lines. Some dictionaries define hybrid vigor, or outbreeding
enhancement, as "heterosis, an increased strength of different characteristics in hybrids; the possibility to obtain a 'better' individual
by combining the virtues of its parents."

Not all such crossings produce better offspring. Sometimes
certain crossings produce inferior offspring, with hybrids inheriting
traits that would make them unfit for survival. It is only when the
hybrid is superior to its parents that the term "hybrid vigor" is
used. Although Puggles have not been bred to the same extent or
for as long as some other crossbreeds, all indications so far are positive with respect to health, temperament, looks and other factors.
Of course, using only the best, healthiest examples of both parent
breeds will help to ensure that the resulting Puggles remain well
adjusted and healthy, with a lesser incidence of genetic disorders
than the parent breeds.

Given that you have done your homework properly as the new
owner of a Puggle, meaning that you have chosen a puppy that is

a Puggle's best friend is his vet.

A Puggle puppy is full of heart.

healthy, has been examined by your vet and is seemingly free from any troubling maladies, it is time to bring the new puppy home and start him on a program to ensure his future health and well-being. You should have received the puppy's health records when you took him home; this will document all veterinary visits, medications and vaccinations your puppy has received since birth. These records should document the types of vaccinations and wormings and dates administered, along with information on any medications given (including the labels from the bottles, if available). The health records should also have information as to when the next vaccinations are due, as well as any other information or tips that might be helpful to the new owner.

Most eight-week-old puppies have received at least one, or perhaps two, of the series of puppy immunizations necessary to protect against the most dangerous illnesses, including parvovirus, parainfluenza, distemper and canine hepatitis.

These shots are the start of a series of vaccinations. It is necessary for the puppy to receive the entire series in order to have full protection. Although some veterinarians follow a slightly different immunization schedule, these shots are typically given at 6, 8, 10, 12 and 16 weeks of age. If puppies are raised in cities, they should not be taken to public parks or walked on city streets until the entire complement of shots has been given. Puppies under 16 weeks of age are highly susceptible to parvovirus, distemper and various other diseases.

Puppies should be wormed at two, four, six and eight weeks of age for roundworms, parasitic nematodes commonly found in most dogs. Whereas adult dogs may test worm-free, if the mother dog ever had roundworms, even as a puppy, juvenile stages of these worms lie dormant in the mother dog's body tissues. When the mother dog becomes pregnant and certain hormones are emitted into her system, the worms become energized and migrate into the bloodstream, thence traveling to the puppies by way of the umbilical cord. Many puppies are born with worms already in their systems.

There are other types of worms that can invade a puppy's intestinal system as well: hookworms, whipworms, tapeworms and pinworms. Some of these worm types are transmitted from the mother dog. Others are transmitted by mosquitoes (e.g., heartworms), by sniffing or eating feces from dogs who are infected with worms or by finding and eating feces from other animals such as rabbits, deer, etc.

All puppies must have a veterinary health certificate and be at least eight weeks of age before being shipped by air. Some vets give a cursory examination, but it is a good idea for the buyer to ask the seller of the puppy to have the puppy checked by a vet prior to shipping or prior to your picking him up as an added measure of buyer protection. The examining veterinarian should write and sign a letter describing what he has checked for and what was found. You should

Good health shines through in a puppy's expression, coat and overall demeanor.

then follow up with a visit to your vet once puppy is home with you.

While puppies are weaned from their mothers at six weeks of age, and can safely go to their new homes by eight weeks of age, there are exceptions to this rule. Very tiny puppies (under 3 pounds) can be overly stressed by a long plane ride or car trip. Some of these puppies can become hypoglycemic, a condition in which the levels of blood sugar become critically low. Puppies with this condition can succumb and die very quickly. Thus very small puppies should be kept until they reach a higher weight or until they are older, usually 10 to 12 weeks of age, before they go to their new homes.

We have talked about things to look for when selecting a puppy. There are valid reasons for doing this. Dogs can contract a myriad of parasites (e.g., worms, protozoa, mites) and infections in the short time between birth and the age at which they are ready and able to go to their

A healthy, bright-eyed puppy, ready to steal your heart.

new homes. The following can be used by owners as a quick reference guide to aid in choosing a good puppy.

WORMS

Suspect roundworms if the puppies are pot-bellied or have dull coats. Worms take the nutrition out of whatever food the puppy is eating. If a puppy is infested with worms, he will be eating but getting very little of the nutrients needed for growth. Once worms mature (and this happens within a matter of weeks), they fill the puppy's digestive tract in the belly, and the puppy will not feel like eating. Worms also migrate through the puppy's body, entering the lungs and causing coughing. This coughing is sometimes mistaken for kennel cough.

Suspect tapeworms if you see fleas on the puppies. Fleas carry tapeworms. Tapeworms attach to the intestinal lining, feeding on the nutrients being digested by the puppy. Tapeworm segments can also be passed in the feces of adult

All pups in the litter should be in good condition, healthy and well cared for.

dogs and older pups. These motile segments, which look like grains of rice, are actually egg sacs. Dog or puppies sniff the feces or ingest these sacs and become infested or rein-fested with the tapeworms.

Pay close attention to the area where the puppies are housed, and ask to see where they are allowed to go out and play. If these areas are not clean, suspect that the puppies are not getting proper care. The manner in which a puppy starts his life means a great deal. It can be the difference between bringing home a healthy puppy who has a good start and bringing home a sickly puppy who may have permanent damage that will show up later on in life and possibly cause hefty vet bills.

SKIN MITES
Check the puppy's coat and skin. If the hair feels greasy and there is substantial dandruff present, the puppy could be harboring skin mites. Watch the puppies at play or rest. Are any of them scratch-ing? Puppies will scratch if

they have skin mites, mange mites, lice or fleas. Although mange mites are too small to be seen without a microscope, signs like severe dandruff and a dull or greasy-feeling coat can be indicative of an infestation. There are two types of mange: sarcoptic and demodectic. Sarcoptic mange is passed from dog to dog, and the mites can survive off a host for a number of days. It is curable with shampoos, dips and medication. These mites can be passed to humans as well. Demodectic mange is passed on from the dam, and it is more difficult to cure. Suspect demodectic mange if the puppy is very young and exhibits symptoms of mange. This is another very good reason to want to see the dam.

Love your puppy by providing him with the best in healthcare.

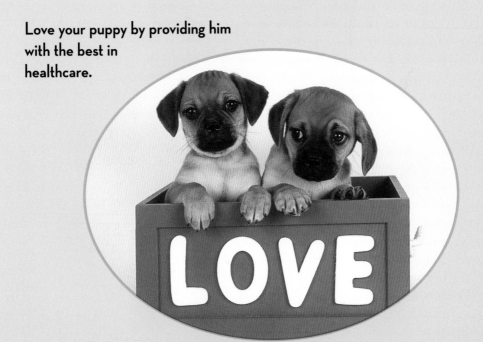

If she is healthy-looking with a shiny coat, clear eyes and a happy attitude, the chances of getting a good, healthy puppy are much better.

PROTOZOA

Plan on spending time when choosing or picking up your puppy. You will want to see your puppy defecate while you are there. Young puppies have numerous bowel movements per day, and the chances are high that your puppy, possibly all of the puppies in the litter, will have bowel movements during playtime. You will want to see that the puppy's stool has a firm shape with no signs of diarrhea or blood. Never take home a puppy if you suspect or see that the puppy has diarrhea. No reputable seller would allow a puppy to leave the premises if the pup has diarrhea, is vomiting or is coughing. Blood in the stool can signify worm infestation or other conditions brought on by protozoa in the intestinal tract.

Protozoa are one-celled organisms that invade the intestinal tract, multiply rapidly and cause bloody or gelatinous stools. One of these protozoa is called *Coccidia*; another is *Giardia*. Both are water-borne and can be picked up from ground water, well water, an infected mother dog or infected surroundings. These protozoa are insidious. They cannot be seen, and sometimes puppies can harbor them and show no

Welcome to the beginning of a long and happy friendship with your healthy Puggle!

outward signs of carrying them. A strong, healthy puppy can, and will, develop resistance to these protozoa. Puppies weakened from lack of good food, from being infested with worms, from being stressed out due to shipping or from going to new homes and becoming overtired from not getting enough rest can succumb to protozoan infection and become very ill or die. Many breeders routinely give medication for coccidian protozoa if they think there is a chance that their pups or adult dogs might harbor them. If you are given medicine for your new puppy, suspect that the puppy has one of these conditions. Albon is the medicine of choice for *Coccidia*; Flagyl is the medicine given for *Giardia*. Both medicines are extremely effective.

SPAYING/NEUTERING

Other important considerations are spaying and neutering. As Puggles are not used for breeding and are bought as family pets, they should be spayed (if female) or neutered (if male).

There are many vets and breeders who feel that without doing these procedures, dogs are more prone to diseases. Of course this is true and it makes sense. If a female dog has no uterus, she cannot succumb to uterine cancer or ovarian cancer. She will be much less likely to get cancer of the mammary glands as well. Male dogs that are neutered cannot get testicular cancer.

There are other valid reasons for spaying or neutering. Although we all think that we can watch over our dogs constantly, this is not always the case. Intact male dogs tend to roam. Intact female dogs must be constantly watched over during estrus so they do not get together with a male dog. Females remain in season for up to three weeks. This can occur twice a year. As a pet owner, it is far easier to not have to deal with these things. A responsible seller will try to steer new owners toward spaying or neutering their new puppy; some will even have a spay/neuter clause in their sales agreement.

House-training brings BIG

House-training Your
Puggle

House-training begins the moment you bring your Puggle home. As with dieting, it's not something that's done for only a couple of days—it's a lifestyle for quite a while. Until good habits are formed, you must be diligent and consistent. As the appropriate habits become ingrained within your Puggle, you'll be able to decrease your diligence as the dog expands his control and communication abilities.

As with all dogs, care must be taken to maintain a schedule for feeding and relief. Scheduling and consistency are how dogs learn. They have spectacular internal clocks that automatically affect their

A "snuggle Puggle" is in his element with a cozy bed and a cuddly littermate.

rewards for puppy and owner.

physical functions. If your Puggle knows at what times he's going to eat and go outside, he can learn to control his bodily functions far faster. With consistency, your Puggle can be house-trained in less than a week!

Due to the sensitivity of your Puggle, you'll want to avoid creating negative associations with any learning experience. Positive reinforcement and redirection are the keys to training success. Always show your dog how to perform correctly. Don't rely upon punishment for incorrect responses. Improper behavior happened because you did not properly guide and reinforce your pup. In other words, bad behavior did not occur because your puppy was being vindictive, hateful or stupid. Puggles can be willful, but dogs don't

Boundaries and supervision are essential to a pup's safety and good behavior.

"I'm
dressed,
my leash is on
and I am
waiting...what more
of a hint do you need?"

Communication is the key to seeing eye-to-eye with your Puggle.

hold grudges. Undesirable behavior occurs because of your lack of clear communication.

LET'S TALK

Let's begin with some very basic communication skills: vocal tones and visual cues. Using these will help bridge the language barrier between you and your Puggle. When using your voice, there are three distinct tones that have meaning to your dog: a high, happy, enthusiastic tone, to be used when praising; a demanding tone, to be used when giving a command; and a low growly tone, to be used when reprimanding.

Keeping your volume down maintains the tones' meanings. Raising your voice confuses the communication, so never shout, scream or yell. Your dog will not ignore you if you are consistent and clear. If your Puggle understands what is being said and knows that good things happen when he listens, then you will get the proper response from your little dog.

At least 70 percent of a canine's communication is through visual movement/body language. Each body part that your dog moves has many nuances. Since we don't have moveable ears or tails or the ability to secrete scent when we wish, we'll have to rely on two basic positions that our dogs will understand: dominant and submissive. The dominant position is when you are standing or sitting upright. The submissive position is when you are crouched down or lying on the floor. When giving a command or corrective tone, the dominant position will relay your message more effectively. When greeting your dog, playing with him or releasing him from work, the submissive position is best.

How does this help house-training? Immensely. Once you can communicate with your Puggle, he'll learn the house rules faster, knowing he'll be rewarded for doing so.

SCHEDULING

Dogs are creatures of habit. Once given an idea of what will happen and when, your Puggle will gladly adhere to what you want.

Schedule your dog's feeding times. A young puppy should eat three times a day, let's say 6 a.m., 12 p.m. and 5 p.m. (or whatever works with your schedule). A Puggle puppy over five months of age can eat twice a day, morning and evening. Put his food bowl down at the given times and be sure to pick up any uneaten food after ten minutes. This teaches your Puggle pup to eat at allotted times, not throughout the day. Having a feeding schedule will greatly help with house-training, as eating at regular times means he will also have to relieve himself at regular times.

Now for the potty trips. Choose a specific spot in which you want your Puggle to relieve himself. This can be outdoors or in an indoor litter box. When you take your dog to his relief spot, always go the same way. If the relief area is outdoors, always leave the house with your Puggle through the same door and go to that spot. If indoors, always traverse the same path to the litter box location. The less you vary, the faster your pup will learn and the sooner he'll be able to let you know when it is time to relieve himself.

Next, establish the words you will use to cue your Puggle pup. Be sure everyone in the household uses the same words. Some examples are: "Potty," "Hurry," "Outside" and "Business." There are also phrases you can use to alert your Puggle that the two of you are on your way out the door for his relief time, such as "Let's go outside." This, paired with your actions of going to the door, gives your pup a clear definition of what is happening and what is expected of him. The best way to ensure that your pup learns his potty word is to be sure to use it at times when you are certain he's going to relieve himself, such as first thing in the morning or after a meal. Puggles love to learn new things and should pick up on the word within a week.

Bring a special treat with you when you go outside or to the litter box with your pup. This treat is reserved specifically for potty success. As soon as your Puggle has completed

HERE'S A SAMPLE SCHEDULE TO GET YOU STARTED

6 a.m.: Take him outside or to his litter box. Tell him his relief word over and over until he goes. As soon as he goes, praise him. If he needs to do more, hold off on giving him the treat until he is finished. Female dogs tend to get their business over with more quickly than male dogs.

6:30 a.m.: Feeding time. Make sure your dog finishes his meal within the time allotted. Whether he has finished or not, after ten minutes pick up his food dish. Always leave fresh water available. Keep an eye on your pup. If he begins to sniff and circle, get him to his relief area as soon as possible. Even without these cues, take him to his area within 15 minutes. Remain with him and give him his potty word over and over until he goes. Praise and reward.

If your Puggle is under four months of age, make sure you get him to his relief zone every 60-90 minutes. Also, if he is eating three times per day, this more frequent feeding schedule will increase his need to relieve himself. Remember to keep him in his relief area until he goes. He should have to urinate. Most dogs defecate twice a day, but pups might need to do so three or four times per day. Be aware of your pup's habits and be certain to get him to his relief area at the appropriate times.

12 p.m.: For pups 5 months and under, feed and take him to his potty area 15 minutes later. Continue taking him out every 60-90 minutes. Older pups should have a potty trip.

5 p.m.: Feed and take out 15 minutes later.

7 p.m., 9 p.m. and 11 p.m.: Go outside. Using the potty word, make certain he does his business and then reward him.

A dog-
proofed
room with
an easy-to-
clean floor
can provide
safe
confinement
for your
Puggle.

relieving himself, give him praise and the reward. The treat doesn't always have to be food. Puggles love to play and receive attention. A game of fetch or a belly rub can be just as rewarding. Regardless of the reward, you should always use very enthusiastic praise when-ever your pup relieves himself outside. This reinforces his actions in the correct place, making him desirous of performing the behavior another time.

If your Puggle is under four months of age, he will need to relieve himself very often: after sleeping, within 15 minutes of eating and during playtimes. Keep these times in mind.

Feeding time is scheduled, so you'll know when to take him outside after eating, but your pup doesn't always stick to a specific time of day for naps and play. You'll need to be aware of what your pup is doing and react accordingly.

CRATE TRAINING

Crate training can be extremely helpful during house-training, especially if you cannot watch your dog every minute or if you are not at home during the day. How realistic is it to observe your pup around the clock? Not very. Teaching him to remain in the crate when you cannot watch him has several benefits:

1. It helps teach your Puggle to control himself. It is instinc-tive for a dog to not relieve himself in his den. However, if you obtained your Puggle at a pet store, there is the chance that he had no choice but to soil his cage. Regardless if the cage had a grated floor or solid floor, the habit is instilled. This dog might require more diligent observation and more oppor-tunities to go to his relief

area than a dog that was raised by a breeder.

2. Crating keeps your dog out of trouble when you cannot be with him. He cannot wander around the house, getting into danger or mischief.

3. Due to its den-like atmosphere, it gives your dog comfort. Many people don't like the idea of putting their young dogs into crates. This is a very human attitude, as we dislike being confined. Dogs, however, if left alone, will search out small places to curl up and lie down in. In the wild, dogs will always search out dens in which to bear their young or maintain their own safety. They like feeling something solid all around them, as it gives them a sense of security. This instinct is still very strong in domestic dogs. Puggles love to feel something surrounding them. They'd prefer it to be you—your bed, lap, arms— but they'll easily accept a soft bed inside a crate.

4. The crate is a place of retreat for your dog when he

Cozy bedding and toys help a Puggle feel at home in his crate.

is feeling overwhelmed or tired. If he doesn't wish to be in the middle of commotion or is tired, he will retreat to his safety zone.

Begin crate training from day one. Put your pup's bed, food and water in the crate. Add several toys, especially interactive ones such as food-filled bones or hollow rubber toys, soft squeaky toys and toys that both massage his gums and maintain his attention. All these things make the

HOW TO TEACH YOUR PUP TO GO INTO HIS CRATE ON COMMAND:

1. Sit near the crate and play with your pup.
2. Throw a toy or treat into the crate. Praise your Puggle as he retrieves the reward. Repeat this three to five times.
3. When your pup is comfortable moving in and out of the crate, briefly close the door. Remain sitting near the crate and continually praise him. Stick a treat through the openings so that your pup remains positive about the experience. Open the door and allow your pup to come out.
4. Gradually increase the time that your Puggle is in the crate as you remain next to it. When he lies down and makes himself comfortable, leave the room for a short period of time—say five minutes.
5. As long as your Puggle doesn't fuss, whine or scratch, return, give him a treat and open the door. If he does fuss, return and wait until he stops, then reward him and open the door. Try again. Repeat this process until your Puggle pup is comfortable and quiet.
6. Gradually increase the time that your pup is left in the crate with you out of the room. When he is quietly comfortable for upward of half an hour, you can increase his crate time in half-hour increments. Within a week or less he should be able to be left safely in his crate for 4-6 hours.

crate an enticing room, much like one for your child. What child wouldn't want a room that has a comfortable bed and is loaded with toys and goodies?

The crate can also help you with house-training by teaching puppy not to play and procrastinate when you take him on a potty trip. If you take him out to potty and he does not do so within ten minutes, return inside and put him in his crate for half an hour. He can have his toys and soft bed. He merely cannot have more freedom within your home where he might end up relieving himself.

Yes, this is a means of punishment for not doing as you requested, but it is not a harsh punishment, merely a psychological one, as ostracizing is a normal dog-pack correction for insubordination. The crate should never be used for "time-out" punishment, as this would make it an undesirable place for your Puggle. You also should never scold your dog as you are

A dog's crate is his castle.

when he takes it. Repeat this a few times. You can be sure he'll remain very close to the bell at this point.

Now you need to wait until he makes the move without your luring him. He'll go to sniff the bell to see if you "accidentally" dropped some treats you haven't pointed out to him. When he does, praise and reward him. At first he'll just look at you, wondering what he did to earn that reward. It will soon dawn on him to go check out the bell again. After all, it yielded rewards in the past. When he does so, praise and reward him again. By this time you'll see the little light bulb over his head turn on. He will go to the bell and push at it with his nose. Again, praise and reward. The next time, however, make sure he makes the bell ring. No praise or reward until he does so. As soon as he makes it ring, give him a treat and take him outside. Repeat this process each time you take him outside. With each successive session, he will make fewer

and fewer mistakes, making a more concentrated effort to ring the bell.

How much clearer can it be that your dog needs to go outside?

INDOOR RELIEF TRAINING

If you live in a high-rise or other type of compact community, you may not want to take your Puggle outdoors to relieve himself. Not only will it take longer to reach his relief zone (and he may not be able to hold it that long), but a young pup may pick up germs and bacteria in public places before he is fully vaccinated. Also, a Puggle's Pug ancestry makes him prone to respiratory problems and difficulty regulating his body temperature in extreme weather, so having an indoor potty zone will be helpful in maintaining his health and well-being. Besides, it's often very inconvenient to have to take your dog outdoors to potty when there's a snow storm blowing outside or when the summer heat and humidity are beyond the comfort zone.

Begin by obtaining some house-training pads, which are already treated with an attractive scent, making it highly likely that your Puggle pup will want to use them. There are frames that hold these pads in place while also protecting your floor. To make certain the area is clearly delineated, I'd suggest placing an exercise pen around the pad with the door left open for your Puggle to go through. This potty zone should be set up near an area where you and your dog spend most of your time so that it's readily available when your Puggle has the need.

"Can I have some privacy, please?"

Follow the same procedures as outlined for outdoor training, but always take your dog to his indoor potty zone and close the pen so that he can't leave until he's relieved himself. The moment he does so, praise, reward and allow him out of the pen. Always keep in mind, however, that male dogs tend to have to go more than once in a single trip, and many dogs will have to both urinate and defecate first thing in the morning and later in the afternoon. Make sure your dog is completely finished with his business before allowing him the freedom of your home. This will prevent accidents and help house-training to be achieved more quickly.

Bright, alert and ready to learn...

Obedience Training for Your
Puggle

Puggles are intelligent but willful, and some can be stubborn. They're cute little dogs that are fun to play and snuggle with, but they need to learn to behave just like all other dogs or they won't be a pleasure to have around. You must always keep in mind that small dogs are still *dogs*, not stuffed toys or ornaments. Puggles are living, breathing creatures who have a natural social order.

Training needs to be approached in a positive, rewarding, clear and consistent manner. This breed does not learn well with force or harsh treatment; in fact, this can totally turn them off, causing many to retreat into another room or their crates or to just roll over onto their backs, showing their tummies in an "I give up" gesture. On the other hand, if an exercise is broken down into small components and clearly defined, your Puggle will quickly learn whatever you wish to teach him.

Other than for adornment, I suggest not using a neck collar of any sort on your Puggle. The best tool for training and walking your toy dog is an Easy Walk or Sensation harness. It wraps around your dog's front end with the leash attachment at the chest, so that you can easily turn him without choking him in any manner if he moves away from you. I wouldn't recommend a regular harness that has a leash attachment at the back/shoulder area, as the dog will merely pull harder when he feels any tension from you. Have you

your Puggle will amaze you.

Your Puggle will be alert to the sound of the clicker once he learns that "click" means "reward."

ever seen dogs pulling a sled? If you use a regular harness, that will be your Puggle pulling you down the street.

As mentioned, the best training approach is through positive reinforcement. This is done with a reward, such as food, a toy or touch, and with something to "mark" the moment the dog does something you wish him to do, such as praising with the word "Good" or "Yes." You can also use a clicker to mark the moment your Puggle performs correctly. A clicker is a small rectangular box that makes a distinct noise. Regardless of the type of noise or word you use to mark the moment of a correct behavior, be consistent with it.

Before you begin, make a list of the things you ultimately wish to teach your Puggle. While having him perform magnificent tricks is great, it's always best to begin with the basic behaviors: sit, stay, down and come. Once these four foundation actions are understood, you can build on them to accomplish whatever goals you set for your dog. It would also be a good idea to teach your Puggle how to walk on a loose leash, as this will be necessary for your everyday routine.

Begin by taking your dog into a quiet area where there are no distractions—no other animals, no toys, no extraneous noise. Since they have hunting hound blood from their Beagle ancestry, Puggles are highly perceptive of every smell and movement around them. You'll initially accomplish far more by working in a quiet environment where your dog can concentrate on you instead of distractions. Once your Puggle has an understanding of an exercise, you can gradually expose him to distractions as you work with him so that he learns to perform regardless of where he is and what is going on around him. Imagine your Puggle walking at your side while passing another dog. Now that's good training!

We need to establish that the word "Good" or "Yes" (I'll use "Good" for sake of consistency) means that he is doing something well and will receive a reward. If you are using another type of marker, such as a clicker or squeaker (yes, squeaky toys work well here, too) be sure to pair the sound of the tool with the moment your Puggle performs as you wish. Pairing the reward with the word "Good" and/or the sound of a click is a "bridging signal." This means that the sound acts as a bridge between your dog's good behavior and his receiving his reward. Give your dog a treat as you use your bridging signal in order to teach him that the two are paired together.

The next exercise is called targeting. Your dog must learn to watch a specific object in order to earn his reward. The easiest object is your hand, as

"Misbehave? Us? Never!"

Consistency... the Key

If your dog learns what to expect and when it will occur, he will learn faster. Pairing specific vocal and language cues with a particular behavior will quickly teach your dog the meaning of your cues. The same cues will need to be used for a given behavior regardless of the situation. Changing the cues when there are distractions present will merely confuse your dog. Expecting less of your dog in the presence of distractions will also teach him that you don't wish for him to respond in certain situations.

Consistency, regardless of where you are and what is going on around you, will ensure clear communication and reliable, correct responses to your commands.

he'll need to learn specific hand cues for each exercise. Place a piece of food in your hand and show it to your Puggle. When he touches your hand, praise or click and give him his reward. Repeat this a couple of times until your dog is eagerly moving to your hand.

You can move your hand up, down and side-to-side. Each time you do, your Puggle should follow your hand with his nose. As he watches the target, praise him in a high, happy, enthusiastic tone of voice. When you are done with the action, give him a reward. Be sure he was able to follow your hand in all directions. If he shows confusion, back up to a more simple movement and make sure he's readily responding to it before making the movement more complicated. Sometimes you need to regress a little in order to progress to the next level. Pushing ahead before your dog is ready will only cause frustration for both of you. Take your time and do it right, giving your Puggle a chance to learn in a positive way.

The food-motivated Puggle will pay attention when a treat's at stake.

COME AND SIT

Once your Puggle knows how to target, we can teach him to come and sit. Begin by showing him the target to get his attention. Hold your hand in front of your knees, making sure that your dog can see your hand and smell the treat inside. If your Puggle is a Pocket Puggle, you might want to lower the target to your shins; if he can't see and smell the target, he won't have much interest in moving toward it.

As he moves his nose toward your hand, go backward two steps. He will come toward you. When he does so, praise/click and give him his reward. The next time, take a few more steps backward, always luring your Puggle to come toward you.

dog's head and between his eyes. As he looks upward at his target, his rear end will lower. As soon as his rear end touches the floor, praise and give your Puggle his reward. After two repetitions, add the word "Sit" as you lure your dog into position.

As some Puggles can be a bit stubborn, you may have to place your dog into position if he pretends to not understand the sit command. Some of these little dogs just don't want to make themselves appear any smaller, as they believe they should be large and in charge.

If you must place your Puggle into a sit, continue to target his head upward with one hand as you press gently on his bottom to lower it with the other hand. Since he's small, you might have the best luck if you crouch or kneel so that you don't have to reach down so far, which can be a bit threatening to the dog.

Once he readily sits on command, you can bring the two commands, come and sit,

After three or four repetitions, you should be going backward at least ten steps as your dog attentively comes toward you. At this time, add the word "Come" as you move backward. As your Puggle is rewarded for his response, he will begin to associate this word with the action of coming toward you.

Next we add the sit. This is also easily done through targeting. Merely place your hand (with the treat in it) over your together for a chain of behaviors. A chain of behaviors means more than one behavior prior to his receiving the reward. This is how you can teach your dog to listen to you without giving him a treat for every single thing he does. As he advances his knowledge and communication skills, he will be able to perform many commands before he receives any rewards other than praise. Praise should never be withheld, as your Puggle thrives on hearing this from you.

Your Puggle should learn to come when you call him no matter what he's doing.

HEEL AND SIT

When your Puggle is very comfortable doing the come and sit, you can start teaching him to walk with you. This is called the heel and sit. Instead of your target moving backward with you, it will be moving forward with you. Also, you'll be keeping your target at your side and held low, because that's where you want your dog to be while walking with you. This position prevents your tripping over him and helps him watch you better.

At this point you'll be sure to want to acclimate your Puggle to the Easy Walk or Sensation harness so that you can keep him safely on a leash. This way, if he sees something interesting, you won't lose your dog. This is of great importance when working outdoors.

After doing a come and sit, put yourself at your dog's side. Which side doesn't matter, although most people will walk their dogs on their left. If teaching your Puggle to walk on your left side, be sure to use the visual cue of stepping out on your left leg as you give the heel command. Should your dog walk on your right side, use your right leg first as you give the command. The idea behind this is that having the leg closest to the dog begin moving is a stronger visual cue than having the opposite leg begin moving. The movement will encourage your dog to begin walking with you.

Since your Puggle is now familiar with following the target, you can begin using the word "Heel" on that very first step forward. Keep the target at about knee or shin level where your dog can easily see and smell the reward. Go forward two to five steps, stop and tell your dog to sit. If your target remained at your side, near your knee, your Puggle will also be there, sitting as you had requested. Be sure to praise/click and reward.

If your dog did not move with you, lure him with the treat. Don't go back to him. Once he's reached your side, go forward only two steps, stop, tell him to sit and reward him. Sometimes you need to go a little slower.

When he's able to remain at your side for two to five steps, increase the amount of steps between each stop and sit. Because Puggles have a high food drive, your dog is highly likely to be very close to the target, remaining with you. Once you and he have accomplished 20 steps, incorporate turns and changes of pace. Always keep your target where he can see it, and praise the entire time your dog is moving with you.

With a well-trained Puggle, walks
will be fun for both of you.

Outdoor lessons may be too much for a curious young pup who is likely to be distracted by everything.

When your Puggle can walk with you and come readily, it is time to move your training sessions outdoors or, if you were already in a quiet area outdoors, move to an area that presents minor distractions. The distractions can be as simple as a different surface, such as grass, or they can include dog toys. It's especially helpful if you can get someone to throw the dog toys around while you work with your dog. This helps with the overall distraction-proofing required to do any activity with your Puggle.

Should you live in an apartment building, begin the distraction-proofing in the long hallways. There's sure to be people and maybe even other dogs coming and going, presenting great distraction-proofing opportunities. It's also a chance to show off your cute Puggle to the neighbors!

If there's something that causes your dog to disengage his attention, you'll need to retreat to a point in your training when he was watching you better and be more gradual in introducing the distraction.

Also, you may want to change the reward to something more valuable to the dog. For example, he sees a squeaky toy and wants very much to get the toy instead of watching your target. Obviously, the squeaky toy is more of a reward than the treat. Pick up the toy and use that to target him. After a few heel and sit or come and sit repetitions, let him mouth and play with the squeaky toy. Then return to the exercises using his chosen reward. However, you'll likely discover that Puggles will be more influenced by food rewards than toys. If there is a situation in which this isn't the case, reconsider the type of food reward you're using. Also, it's best not to have a training session directly after a meal, as his food drive will be very low. Generally, a great food reward is freeze-dried liver, cheese (though not great amounts of it) or little pieces of cooked chicken.

When approaching something that distracts your Puggle, the best way to regain his attention is to turn in the opposite direction. When he is once more watching you, have him sit and reward him. It may take a while to walk around the block, or even all the way down the hall, but your dog must learn to do so on a loose leash, not pulling you along. Be sure that your Puggle receives his reward for moving forward on a loose leash, not by pulling.

SIT AND STAY

When your Puggle is reliable with the come, sit and heel exercises, it's time to begin the stay exercise. This might be difficult for a young Puggle, but very comfortable for a dog over the age of one year. You see, puppies have a difficult time staying still for more than a few seconds, while an older dog prefers to remain still and observe his surroundings.

To build a solid stay, you need to break the exercise down into three components: time, movement and distance. Later, once all these elements are accomplished, you can add distraction-proofing as well.

We'll start by discussing the time factor, which is added very gradually, beginning with only

Controlling Bad Behavior with Commands

After your Puggle (and you) have learned the four basic commands, it will become so much easier for you to control any bad behaviors that your puppy or dog may exhibit, such as jumping on people, jumping on furniture, running out the front door, etc. A dog cannot be doing two behaviors simultaneously! If a dog jumps up on a guest who just came into your home, using the sit command will immediately have your dog sitting instead of jumping. If a visitor is fearful of dogs, giving your dog the down/stay command will make the dog seem far less threatening.

two seconds and aiming for the goal of one minute. Begin by working on the behaviors with which your dog is familiar: heel, sit and come. Next, stop and have your dog sit at your side. Prior to giving him his reward, which signals the end of the exercise, put your hand in front of his face with your palm facing him and give the command "Stay." If your dog is easily distracted, don't move...yet. If he's comfortable with remaining still for a few seconds, step in front of him using the leg you don't use first for the heel command.

If working with a pup under six months of age or with an insecure dog, go ahead and target your dog as he remains in the sit/stay. The target should be held steady, just above his nose, so that your dog doesn't move. As he remains in place, praise him. Return back to the heel position (by your dog's side) and reward him as you continue to praise. This first attempt should not last more than a few seconds at best. You want to set up your Puggle for success, not failure, so set parameters in which your dog

"All of this learning is exhausting!"

will perform correctly and build from there.

While your Puggle remains in place, be sure to praise him. Don't get super giddy with the praise, just be enthusiastic that your dog is performing. Puggles love to be praised, but if you get him too excited he won't be able to remain in the stay position.

The next time you attempt the stay command, add a few more seconds before returning to the heel position and rewarding your dog. Sometimes it's difficult to know exactly how long you are maintaining the stay. I usually count in "Good dogs" (or "Good girls" or "Good boys"). It takes about a second to say this and, as your dog gets better at the stay command, you just keep adding "Good dogs." Eventually, after about 20 "Good dogs," it becomes more of a tongue twister than a form of praise, so you can tone it down to a "Good dog" every couple of seconds. Just be certain to maintain an enthusiastic, yet not a "baby-talk," vocal tone.

There might be times when your Puggle will attempt to get out of remaining in place.

This will happen more and more often if you don't acknowledge his behavioral thresholds. A behavioral threshold is the period of time for which your dog can maintain a specific behavior. If he moves out of position, it means his threshold has been breached. You've attempted to make him remain in place longer than he is able to at that time. Should this happen, back up to the amount of time for which your dog was successful. For example, at around 20 seconds your dog moves out of his stay. However, during the previous attempt at 15 seconds, he remained in place. Go back to the 15-second stays for a while and then gradually work up to the 20-second period. If a five-second increase is too much, do a two- or three-second increase.

When your Puggle moves before he should, always return him to the position in which he was originally. You can either lure him there with your target (which is the easiest way, unless he's distracted) or you can guide him there with the use of a leash.

Once he's back in place, reiterate the stay command and return to his area of comfort. Puggles can be very willful, especially if there's something else they'd rather be doing, but they also can be easily intimidated or flustered. Take your time and train in a methodical and positive way.

Trained Puggles are delightful companions in the home.

This will ensure that your dog fully understands each step of the exercise prior to proceeding to the next level.

Once you've accomplished increasing the time for which your dog stays, you can add the next factor, movement. Begin to move around your dog, still remaining close enough to touch him. You'll go from standing in front of him to moving along his sides to eventually going all the way around him.

Begin by stepping side to side in front of him. Keep your leash loose and, if your dog has a tendency to scoot in your direction, keep the target directly over his nose. As he learns to remain still while you move, you can gradually increase the distance between the target and the dog.

While you step from side to side, remain close enough to touch your Puggle on the head. A common error at this point is to move backward. This is rushing ahead and setting up your Puggle for failure. Remember, you want to set him up for success, so take it one step at a time. Also, make certain that you don't accidentally step on your little dog. That will make his learning the exercise and trusting you to move around him very difficult. Remain at least one foot away from him while you move around him, being aware of where you place your feet.

When your dog has maintained his sit/stay during the side-to-side movement, progress to moving along both of his sides. Begin with going to his shoulder on each side. As he becomes comfortable with that motion, go toward his hip on each side.

It's okay for your dog to move his head to watch you and wag his tail to express himself, but he can't scoot his rump around to keep an eye on you. Should he do so, place him back into the correct spot and reiterate the stay command, complete with the visual cue of holding your hand in front of his face.

The next step is to move completely around your Puggle. As your dog targets on your hand, keep your hand still as you walk around your dog. If you move your hand, you move the dog. Keep your hand still and your dog remains still. Should your Puggle be at the point where he doesn't require direct targeting, keep your hands above your waist as you move around him. Always praise enthusiastically as he remains still.

After accomplishing one time around, go for two, then three and so on. Be sure to move around in both directions or you'll get dizzy and your dog will learn to accept your movement in only one direction. Change your direction and teach your Puggle to accept any movement around him.

If using a clicker to bridge the stay, do the click when the stay exercise is complete, not during it. You should praise during the exercise, but the click signifies the end of an exercise, telling the dog he's about to receive his reward.

When your dog is comfortable with your movement, he'll learn to be comfortable with the last factor, distance. You will increase your distance as you move around him. You should spiral out, gradually increasing your distance from him with each successive stay command until you can walk a complete circle around your Puggle at the end of the leash.

Begin with a stay in which you move around your Puggle in both directions. Make sure he's comfortable with your movement and with the amount of time he must remain in position. You must also make sure that you no longer have to do direct targeting as you move around him; if you must still do this, he's not ready for you to increase your distance. Should he be fully comfortable without seeing his reward, go out a couple of feet as you move around him. Always keep your eyes on him, though not staring into his eyes, and praise him as he remains in position.

As your Puggle learns to accept a distance of two feet, go for three. Each successive time you have him do the sit/stay, add more distance until you reach the end of your leash. Please take note, however, that you should begin training with a 5- or 6-foot leash, not a 20-foot leash. That would be expecting far too much from a beginner. If you are doing this indoors and your Puggle is off-leash, don't go so far away that you can't readily put him back into position if he should get up.

There are so many uses for the stay command, from training your Puggle to stay at the door to teaching him to stand still while being examined or bathed to forming the basis of

Another important word for your Puggle to understand is "No."

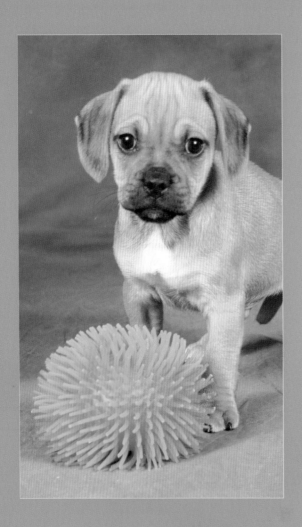

Perhaps a colorful toy is
your puppy's favorite
reward.

many more behaviors and tricks. Once this word is understood, your Puggle will be able to easily learn to stay in any position.

DOWN AND STAY

The difficult part of this exercise is teaching your Puggle to assume the down position on command. Once he's down the stay will be easy, as he already knows the command. He must simply transfer it from the sit position. This association may take a few repetitions, but will soon be understood, provided you take your time and approach all training methodically.

You must make the down exercise pleasant for your dog. It's tough for some dogs to assume a submissive position like the down on command. Your Puggle is no exception. He feels he's already small enough, so why make himself even smaller? Especially when it wasn't his idea to begin with!

The first method you should try is to bait him into position with a treat. This is highly likely to work, as few Puggles can ignore a food reward. You can bait him either from the heel position (beside your dog) or from in front of your dog. You'll probably be more successful standing in the heel position for, should he resist going all the way down, you can easily aid in guiding him. It'll be harder while standing in front of your dog, but since your Puggle isn't large you will still be able to place him in position without too much difficulty. Just be certain not to grab his front legs and pull them forward or he'll stick his rear end up and pull away from you.

A young Puggle pup will likely follow the bait down with no problem. As with the initial sit exercise, it might be helpful to crouch or kneel down to offer you a better means of placing your dog into position without looming over him.

As with everything, there may be a few trouble spots to contend with. Your dog might not be willing to go down all the way. He'll follow the treat with his nose and upper body, but his rear end will remain up. Or he'll move around, trying to

CLICK AND TREAT

Be ready to use lots of treats when clicker training. Dogs of all breeds and mixes will work for rewards. Clicker training has gained popularity as a positive-motivational training method and can be used on any living creature from fish to dog to horse to elephant.

Essentially, the sound of a clicker marks the moment that the animal has performed the correct behavior. As the animal learns that the sound of the click means he'll be receiving a reward, he'll strive to earn the click. If confused, he might perform some random behaviors in the hope of earning the click and subsequent reward.

Those using clicker training should carefully observe their pets and practice moving their thumbs prior to actually using the clicker. Timing is everything.

obtain the reward without putting any part of himself down. The reasons for this vary—anything from not liking the surface you have chosen for this exercise to simply not being willing to put himself in the down position.

To achieve an expedient down, give your Puggle the down command while simultaneously using the target. As he follows the target in one hand, apply pressure just behind his shoulder blades with your other hand. He should easily lower himself. As soon as he does so, praise and give him his reward. Also, release the shoulder pressure and let him up again. I do suggest, however, that you don't just let him up to do whatever he wants. Take him into a forward heel exercise so that his movement remains your idea, under your control.

You can also teach the down with behavior capturing and shaping, but this method requires loads of patience and timely acknowledgment when your Puggle does what you

HAND SIGN LANGUAGE

Just as those with hearing disabilities use sign language to communicate, you can do the same with your dog. As you speak human and Fido speaks canine, the use of hand signals helps bridge the language barrier.

You can use your hand first as a lure, with food, and then as a signal all its own after the dog learns the meaning of each particular gesture.

Hands can give commands.

want him to do. This method, commonly used with clicker training, rewards the dog for "throwing out" behaviors. This means that your dog will constantly be trying things to gain your recognition and rewards. It teaches the dog to reason and think. The only problem is that it's tough to shut it off when you wish without having your dog do a specific requested behavior such as a stay. Some dogs will get the urge to play with you and begin doing things to garner your attention, which might lead to barking because not many people can ignore that.

To accomplish the down command using behavior capturing, you'll need to stand by and observe your dog. You will be watching for your dog to lie down. Always have his rewards handy, for the moment may come at any time and you must be timely in delivering the reward. As soon as he lies down, you'll click/praise and give him his reward. He may

By using the lure, the dog will learn the meaning of the gesture. Within a short time, the gesture alone is all that is needed, while your praise and a treat are rewards for a proper response. Your legs, shoulders and facial expressions can also be utilized to communicate. Dogs are very aware of our most subtle body movements.

Now we're talking!

Hands can give hugs.

stand around for a few minutes, wondering what he did to receive that reward. He'll "throw out" (perform) other behaviors to see if they work. Don't give in. Wait for him to lie down again.

After three to five repetitions, your Puggle will understand. He'll start lying down in front of you every chance he gets. When he does, add the word "Down" to his action. It will take a few more repetitions for him to associate the command with the behavior.

You might need to have your Puggle do a few different exercises in between down commands. This way he won't just lie there, waiting to be rewarded. He learns that the actual action of lying down is what earns him his reward.

Once your dog has an understanding of the down exercise, it's time to teach him to stay in that position, and he's already familiar with the stay command. Before giving the stay command, make certain he's comfortable in the down position. He should be relaxed and not pushing against your hand or scrambling to get up. If he isn't relaxed, try rubbing his ears, chest or tummy. Use slow, calming strokes as you praise him and he should be relaxing into position in no time. You might even find that when he approaches you for attention he drops to the floor and shows you his tummy, ready for a rub.

Begin by gradually increasing the stay time with each successive down command. Remember not to do the down several times in succession, as it will teach your Puggle a pattern instead of attentiveness and obedience. Vary the exercises and keep him guessing what you'll be doing or requesting next.

Instead of stepping in front of him as with the sit/stay, you should first step behind him. If he shows any signs of insecurity, you'll need to bend over and pet him as you move. (Keep in mind that you might want to begin teaching this behavior with your Puggle on a raised platform or crouch down so that you don't have to bend down so far.) This is not easy, but it is necessary for continued positive training while he remains in a socially uncomfortable position.

Once your Puggle is comfortable with your stepping behind him during a down/stay, go to his other side. Continually praise him, petting him if necessary. With each successive down/stay exercise, increase your movement around him. In a very short time you should be able to move entirely around him. If you've been touching him, gradually decrease the amount that you do so as you practice the down/stay exercise. A light touch on his head or side should suffice for a while.

As your dog gains confidence with your movement while he remains in a down/stay, begin gaining a bit of distance. Do this very gradually, as you did with the sit/stay. With each successive stay command, step out a foot or so as you walk around him. Within the same training session that you began moving around your Puggle during the down/stay, you should be able to walk around him at the end of your 6-foot leash.

Be patient and reward your Puggle's progress one small step at a time.

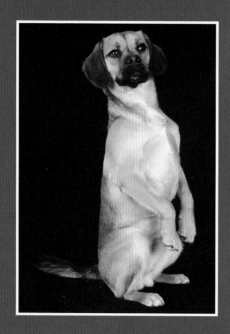

A new twist on the sit command.

COME FROM STAY

Now that your Puggle can stay in both a sit and a down, you can call him to come from either position as well as from his free time. You'll need to practice this exercise from different places around him, ensuring that he will come to you regardless of where you are and what he is doing.

Be aware of anticipation. It's very easy to pattern-train a Puggle. You need only have him perform a chain of behaviors two times in succession. A typical behavior chain is to do a sit/stay and then back up and do a come. Try not to fall into this pattern, as it will extinguish your dog's ability to remain in a stay. He will know that the second you begin to move away from him, he's to get up and come to you. After all, that's when he gets his food reward, isn't it?

Vary the exercises enough to avoid pattern training. Keep him guessing and therefore attentive. Also, never go straight out away from your dog prior to doing a come; it's especially important to never walk straight backwards when either doing a come from a stay or just moving away from your Puggle during a stay. Your "walking backward" movement is signaling to your dog that you are about to call him to come. He'll get up before you even give the command, for he already learned this visual cue when you began his obedience training.

Try putting your Puggle in a stay and walking around him, gradually increasing the distance. As you walk, take out a reward, hiding it a bit so that your dog won't get anxious. Somewhere along the way, turn and face your dog and call him to come. As you call to him, bend forward at the waist to look more inviting. "Reel in" the leash as he comes. Praise him the entire time he is coming to you; this will encourage him as it rewards his actions. Hold the treat where he can see it, about knee height (shin height for the Pocket Puggle) and, as he comes in to you, stand upright. When he arrives, tell him to sit. After he sits, he receives his reward.

You'll have to do a bit of distraction-proofing by "faking him out" every so often. Sometimes, as you move around him, stop and face him but don't call him to come. If he remains in place, praise, return to him and give him his reward. Then tell him to stay again and continue moving around.

The Puggle Performer

You have now completed some basic commands. By no means should you be satisfied with this little bit of knowledge. There is so much more to learn and do with your Puggle. These are mere basics. Your dog is capable of incredible things. As Puggles are clowns by nature, they love learning tricks, especially active ones such as learning to twirl, speak, wave and play dress-up. Since you and he have completed the basic commands together, it will be easy to teach him more words. Puggles love to perform. The more you stimulate yor dog's mind, the better behaved and happier he will be.

The comical and affectionate Puggle

Loving a
Puggle

There's no mistaking the
current popularity of Puggles. They are mentioned and
pictured in newspapers and magazines and have been
featured on *The Oprah Winfrey Show, Live with Regis
and Kelly, The Ellen DeGeneres Show* and major television network
news shows like *The Today Show*. Many celebrities have bought
Puggles and take every opportunity to boast about them. The mere
fact that this hybrid dog is popular among the fashionably elite has
made them even more desirable. Celebrity Puggle owners include
Uma Thurman, James Gandolfini, Sylvester Stallone, Kelly
Osbourne and Jake Gyllenhaal. In fact, Jake and his Puggle Boo
Radley made news when they were among the celebrities who
signed wooden bones for the Mississippi Animal Rescue League's
charity auction. With all of this publicity, Puggles seemed to become
popular almost overnight.

WHAT PUGGLE OWNERS SAY ABOUT THEIR DOGS
Mike Hatton, a Puggle breeder, says, "Among all the different
breeds of dogs/puppies we raise, these little Puggles are our
favorites. We just love them and always hate to see them go. They
are the cutest, best natured, quickest learning and sweetest of all."

Hatton chooses the parents of his Puggles by checking for
good eyes, teeth, conformation and temperament. Hatton says

is so easy to love.

that most Beagles make great mothers and he begins breeding them at a year and a half old. He watches the Beagles very closely for their estrus cycles and puts them with Pug males between the 10th and 15th days of their cycles, recording the first

visual breeding of each pair so that he knows exactly when the puppies should arrive. Though the Beagle moms rarely have problems during the birthing process, they might occasionally need help with the deliveries.

Noting the importance of early socialization, Hatton begins handling the puppies at two to three weeks old, handling them all over and allowing them to lick his face—a favorite Puggle pastime.

Lori Swetland of Hawley, Pennsylvania has nothing but good things to say about her Puggle, Thunderstorm, whom she likens to a mini-Mastiff with his fawn coloring, his black mask and the forehead wrinkles that he never outgrew. He socializes well with her other three dogs—a Jack Russell Terrier and two Chihuahuas. "My Jack Russell Terrier and Thunder play tetherball together," she says. Swetland is amazed at how much Thunderstorm loves playing in the water and at how easy he was to

When it comes to affection, Puggles can't be beat.

train. "He sticks to me like Velcro, following me everywhere."

Her 40-pound Puggle adores playing outside. As he is very food-oriented, he was easy to train, though he was seven months old before being totally reliable with his house-training. Swetland says that having a doggie door helps so that he can go to his outdoor relief area in the fenced yard whenever he needs. At night, Thunderstorm sleeps at Lori's head, as he doesn't ever stray far from her. Lori states, "You can't beat a Puggle for affection and love."

Melody Burton is a professional trainer who met her Puggle through a client who previously owned the dog. She was a dynamo, constantly into everything, not house-trained and unable to sit still. The Puggle's owner gave her up due to allergies. Melody fell in love with this apricot tornado.

Though Melody's Puggle has a heart murmur, the dog doesn't show any signs of the physical ailment as she soars through the agility course, learning all of the obstacles quickly and making great time on the course. "She is learning at lightning speed," Melody says.

Another professional trainer, Nadine Onesti took three Puggles into her home for boarding and training. All three learned very quickly, though they had very high energy levels. They jostled for premium lap-dog posi-

A four-pack of Puggle love.

tions, though never in an aggressive way. The Puggles she worked with were all very affectionate and loving, though two had bouts of cherry eye and the other had skin allergies (both common maladies in Pugs).

Kara Dell'Aquila has worked with several Puggles at her New York-based Kara's Classy K-9s. She states that the male Puggles she's worked with are challenging for their owners to house-train. This occurs most in cases where the male Puggle is the second or third dog introduced into the household. Though neutered, these dogs still marked their territory. She has seen cherry eye in many of the Puggles she's worked with. The dogs often have this corrected when they're under anesthesia for neutering or spaying, though once in a while more than one surgery is necessary to correct the problem.

PUGGLE FUN
Your Puggle can partake in any activity you wish. Even though the purebred registries do not recognize

Mix and Match

The American Kennel Club may thumb its nose at mixed breeds by not allowing them to compete in its sanctioned matches and trials, but there are many other sources for competing in obedience, agility or Rally-O with your dog. Where there's your will, your dog will have fun your way. Don't be intimidated by pure-breed-only trials; seek out other organizations that offer the same types of competition to all dogs.

The United Kennel Club offers titling in Novice, Open and Utility obedience competition. The Association of Pet Dog Trainers offers titling in Rally-O for all dogs, regardless of breeding. The United States Agility Association, the North American Dog Agility Council and the United Kennel Club offer agility competition at all levels for both pure-bred dogs and those of mixed heritage.

Puggles with a fellow short-faced friend, a Boston Terrier.

hybrid dogs, some of them do offer fun matches and competitive performance events for mixed breeds. The American Canine Hybrid Club recognizes Puggles and several hundred other hybrid dog types. In order to be a recognized hybrid, both parents must be registered purebred dogs. Puggles are also allowed to participate in activities sanctioned by the Mixed Breed Dog Club. In addition, there are plenty of activities that Puggles and their owners do just for fun, as well as ways that Puggles can be useful and helpful.

HANDBAG ADORNMENTS

Let's begin with the reason Puggles became an item: they are small dogs with big personalities who do well in apartments and can be easily transported in style. They love to play dress-up, either with ornamental collars (which show well against their short light-colored coats) or outerwear, and they also enjoy being toted in fashionable carriers. A Pocket Puggle will even fit in a large coat pocket. Puggles are hybrid dogs that love to be with people, and they are

Puggles are a kid's best friend!

"Let's play dress-up."

easy to bring along for those dog owners who don't like to leave their dogs at home alone.

AIDES TO THE DEAF

Throughout their history, Pugs have been lifesavers as watch and alert dogs. Puggles inherit this trait; due to this inherent behavior, they work well as hearing assistance dogs, alerting their human companions to things like people at the door, the ringing of the phone or an oven buzzer. Through extensive obedience training and then assistance-dog training, these little dogs can save lives with this important work, alerting their owners to everything from normal daily events to potentially dangerous situations. Don't let anyone tell you that this little toy dog is merely an adornment. A Puggle can fulfill a very important role in his human companions' lives.

"Name that tune."

CHILDREN'S COMPANIONS

Many youngsters feel threatened by dogs. Maybe a child was frightened by a dog that barked and now is apprehensive of all dogs. The Puggle is ideal for the job of being a child's friend and helping the youngster overcome his fear. Plus, a benefit of pet ownership is that it teaches a child responsibility.

Puggles are cute, small and rarely formidable. They are happy to play with anyone; everyone is a friend in a Puggle's eyes. When it is time to rest, the Puggle will happily curl up on a child's lap or sleep beside the youngster at night. This hybrid is great with strangers, so the child's friends will also be welcome.

"Not only am I handsome, but check out my varsity sweater!"

The Puggle is unconditional love in a furry package.

The Puggle is easy to transport, so when the child travels, the dog can come along too. A Puggle companion can be a very positive means of comforting a child whose parents have divorced or if there are other family stresses. Nothing relieves anxiety like a Puggle. Moreover, the more involved the child can be with the training and care of the dog, the more stable that youngster will be in dealing with stress or just the ups and downs of growing up.

THERAPY DOGS

Puggles are ideal therapy dogs. They are easily lifted into a lap, they love to snuggle and cuddle and they have endearing personalities. Because they are easily trained to behave, they can pass the most stringent therapy dog tests and become certified for the job. There are several organizations that offer certification for therapy dogs, including Therapy Dogs International, Inc., Delta Society and Assistance Dogs International. The Delta

Society's website, www.deltaso-ciety.org, has an extensive list of organizations that offer guidance and training for those who wish to become involved in assistance-dog work, including pet-assisted therapy.

Most of the therapy-dog organizations require that the canine candidate have Canine Good Citizen certifi-cation (offered by the AKC for all dogs, purebred and mixed) and extensive obedi-ence training. Also required are a quiet yet outgoing personality and acclimation to service equipment such as wheelchairs, crutches and monitors. To be certified as a therapy dog, the candidate must also be at least a year of age, in good health and up to date on all vaccinations and parasite preventives.

Ready to go on a Puggle puppy picnic?

Puggles are full of life.

Puggle

Resources

The Internet is filled with

Puggle destinations. Most of these sites also offer links to other sites that you might find interesting. Following is a list of the ones I've found to be most helpful.

www.designerdoggies.com
This is the website of professional photographer Chelle Calbert, who owns two Puggles. On this site you'll find information including where to find a Puggle, a list of the recognized hybrid dogs, a link to rescue organizations and information on where to purchase designer-dog merchandise, such as Chelle's marvelous Puggle calendar.

www.dakotawinds.homestead.com
This is the site of a designer dog breeder. This breeder lists lots of information about the dogs she breeds and will help you find the right hybrid for you and your family.

www.Pets4you.com
Pets 4 You is a very large directory for animal lovers. You can see photos of puppies, kittens, dogs and cats as well as other pets for sale. They have one of the most complete lists of breeds and breeders in the US and Canada. They also have a long list of links

fun and surprises!

Living the life of leisure.

www.puggle.org
This site is filled with information about Puggles. It also lists breeders, dogs for sale, dogs in need of rescue, supplies for sale and the latest news about Puggles. A fun feature is that this site allows visitors to submit pictures and video clips of their dogs to share with other Puggle enthusiasts.

www.pugglelove.co.uk
This British site is dedicated to ethical Puggle breeding and ownership, addressing the problems that accompany the hybrid's popularity. Below is an excerpt from their site regarding their careful consideration of Puggles. This is a great site for professional, accurate information about hybrids.

"As part of www.puggle love.co.uk's commitment to ethical breeding, we have sought advice from the Animal Health Trust on the subject of crossbreeding, particularly in relation to Puggles." One of the emails received is shown on the facing page for your information.

for pet supplies, trainers, kennels and more. If you're looking for something that has anything to do with animals, you'll find it here.

www.puggleluv.com
This site offers loads of Puggle information and links to other websites of interest. You'll spend a lot of time here, as there's a lot to read.

Dear Shelley,

Thank you for your email requesting information about the health risks associated with crossbreeding. I lead the genetic research team at the Animal Health Trust and most of my work is involved with investigating inherited diseases that purebred dogs suffer from. So I am well qualified to comment on the issues of crossbreeding.

In a nutshell, purebred dogs suffer from a wide variety of inherited diseases and this is purely a result of the fact that purebred dogs are relatively inbred. This means their parents and their grandparents and in fact all their relations are more related to one another than, say, a human's relatives would be. And that means they share more of their genes, and more of their genetic mutations. It is also why purebred dogs tend to look very much alike—they share a lot of their genetic material, be it good or bad.

Crossbred dogs have parents that are obviously not related to one another, because they are from different breeds—so, from a genetic health point of view, this is A VERY GOOD THING!!! I cannot stress this enough—the more unrelated a dog's parents are, the more healthy it should be. To take this to extremes, mutts (whose parents themselves might be crossbreeds) are the healthiest dogs of all. They might all look different, but they don't suffer from inherited diseases. Crossbred dogs are also unlikely to have the extreme features that some purebred dogs have (the extremely short faces of the Pug, for example, or the very large head of the Bulldog or the very drooping eyes of the Basset Hound) and therefore be more functional and have fewer health issues relating to extreme body type.

I am not saying that crossbred dogs will never get sick, but they are unlikely to suffer from inherited conditions because most mutations that cause inherited conditions are recessive, so a dog has to inherit an identical mutation from both its parents. Pugs and Beagles will each have their fair share of mutations but the mutations that the two breeds have are likely to be different, so a Puggle is unlikely to inherit two copies of the same mutation and is therefore unlikely to suffer from a recessive disease. Dominant diseases are different—these are diseases caused by mutations that only have to be present in a single copy before they cause disease. So if a Puggle inherits a dominant mutation from either of its parents, it will still suffer from that condition. But on the whole, crossbred dogs will be WAY more healthy than purebred dogs.

I hope this helps but if you have any more questions or comments please feel free to contact me directly.

Cathryn Mellersh Ph.D.

P.S. To prove I feel strongly about this crossbreed issue—my dog is a complete mutt!!

We hope you've enjoyed this up-close and personal look at the Puggle!

www.dogbreedinfo.com
Have a question about any hybrid dog, or purebred dog for that matter? This is the site for you. This is the site owner's summary of what the site contains:

"This site is designed to make it easy. Whether it is finding that perfect dog that fits your lifestyle, or that bit of information you need to know, you will probably find it here. If you just love dogs, you will love browsing through the many breed pages and tons of photos that are listed. Choosing a dog should not be taken lightly. There are many different breeds with many different personalities and needs. This site is packed with information on breeds from all groups in an easy to follow format. And new breeds are being added on a regular basis. From detailed breed information, to care articles, to amazing dog photos and even a breed selector and a breeder listing, Dog Breed Info Center® has it all!! A truly extensive collection of all information and guidance for the new, not so new and experienced dog owner."

www.pugglespace.com
You've probably heard of MySpace. Well this is the MySpace for Puggles. This is the website for Puggle owners who want to share photos of and experiences with their beloved pets. If you own a Puggle or plan on getting one, have a look at this site.

www.raineycreekkennel.com
Mike Hatton is a breeder in west central Arkansas who breeds several types of pure-bred toy dogs and hybrid dogs, including Puggles. The pups are raised on a 140-acre farm surrounded by Ouachita National Forest. His site is filled with information about his breeding practices, the dogs he produces and other helpful information.

There are more websites available than I can list in this book. If you go to one, there will be links to others. I do suggest that you read all the information you can about Puggles before buying one. They are not the right dog for everybody. They may be small and cute, but they are willful and filled with energy. You'll need to give a Puggle lots of training, exercise and time. This is a dog who loves company, both canine and human.

Do your research if a Puggle is part of your future plans.

INDEX